# So You Want to Run for Office?

## What You Should Know if You Want to Run for Office or Manage a Political Campaign

By

**Jeff Gold**

So You Want to Run for Office? What you should know if you want to run for office or manage a political campaign

Published in the United States by BCG Publishing, 2020.

www.BCGPublishing.com

# Table of Contents

To those who I could never thank enough for your unconditional support, whether I won or lost: my wife Shawn, Dave, Fitz, Dad, and my mom, Anna B. Gold, who was there in spirit the whole time. I am forever indebted to each of you.

# Disclaimer

The following viewpoints in this book are those of Jeff Gold. These views are based on his personal experience over the past fifty-four years on the planet Earth, especially while living in the politically fueled state of Florida.

The intention of this book is to share his story about what you should know if you are considering running for public office or managing a political campaign.

All attempts have been made to verify the information provided by this publication. Neither the author nor the publisher assumes any responsibility for errors, omissions, or contrary interpretations of the subject matter herein.

This book is for entertainment purposes only. The views expressed are those of the author alone and should not be taken as expert instruction or commands. The reader is responsible for his or her future action. This book makes no guarantees of future success. However, by following the steps that are listed in this book the odds of being more educated in running for office or managing a political campaign are much higher probability.

Neither the author nor the publisher assumes any responsibility or liability on the behalf of the purchaser or reader of these materials.

The views expressed are based on his personal experiences within the political and corporate world, education, and everyday life.

"It is not the critic who counts; not the man who points out how the strong man stumbles, or where the doer of deeds could have done them better. The credit belongs to the man who is actually in the arena, whose face is marred by dust and sweat and blood; who strives valiantly; who errs, who comes short again and again, because there is no effort without error and shortcoming; but who does actually strive to do the deeds; who knows great enthusiasms, the great devotions; who spends himself in a worthy cause; who at the best knows in the end the triumph of high achievement, and who at the worst, if he fails, at least fails while daring greatly, so that his place shall never be with those cold and timid souls who neither know victory nor defeat."

*Theodore Roosevelt, 1910*

# Podcast Invitation

I want to invite you to listen to the Running for Office podcast. We speak with elected officials, managers, strategists, marketing experts, and others involved in the election process. Whether you are a local candidate running for office, a manager of a state or federal campaign, or running for president, join us for tips and techniques to help your particular campaign.

# Introduction

Many people believe that running for public office is easy. You put up some signs, you shake some hands and then you're elected. This may be possible in an election of a small town or an election that is unopposed. In all reality, running for public office is one of the most stressful events of a person's life. I have run for public office twice. I lost my first attempt by just over 1,000 votes and I won my second attempt by a significant majority. For my entire adult life, I worked for elected officials in one form or another and have served in many different positions throughout their campaigns. After the loss of my first election, I came up with a phrase that I tell people who want to run for office or think they know everything about winning an election. That phrase is, "You don't know what it's like to run for office until you have actually done it."

I have been involved in probably a dozen different campaigns as I closed in on my third decade of government service. Some of the elections I was an outsider looking in and in at least two, I was very involved. When you're working in government, it is not a good thing to be on the wrong side of an election, and I found this out the hard way. I kept my job, but it wasn't easy. The one thing I learned was that I wanted to be in the elected position myself one day and vowed to myself not to punish those who did not support me. After my win, I embraced those who openly did not support me, and I believe it has been a positive working relationship for all involved.

In addition to working on my own campaigns and other local, state, and federal campaigns in various volunteer positions, I had the honor of growing up in a household that was very involved in politics. My grandfather was the mayor of a well-known city during his era and my mom was immensely involved in all levels of politics for her political party. Politics were a way of life in the Gold family.

I am not a political strategist and I do not have degrees in political science. In fact, my degrees are in public safety, business, and I have doctoral studies in marketing, healthcare, and education. I respect all who educate themselves, and though a political science degree has not specifically interested me, I enjoy learning from those who have educated themselves in this topic. I have been lucky enough to surround myself with people who had the political knowledge that I am going to pass on in this book, and I will not be able to give credit to everyone.

This book is a collection of what I have learned in over thirty years of government and political service. Being a person who researches everything, I quickly realized there were no guides to running for office or coveted playbooks to follow. In addition to being an avid researcher, I am also a fervid note taker, so I have volumes of journals and date books with notes and comments. Even an internet search of ideas mostly produces links to political strategists and consulting firms. Even though there are many people who are more than willing to tell you what you need to do to win or to run a campaign, the best way is from experience. Unfortunately, not everybody gets the lifetime of experience in the political arena that I have.

The following chapters are a collection of experiences and techniques that I have learned mostly from firsthand experience and experiences from others. There are several references to Florida politics, specifically because this is where I currently serve, but there is no other state that has had the "experiences" that Florida has had in elections. These experiences have included "hanging chads," counting controversies, and other significant events that impact politics around the nation. Though Florida is used as an example often, the tips and techniques mentioned here are useful in any election, from local town elections all the way up to the top offices in the nation.

# Chapter 1

# Why?

The first thing that you will be asked when you decide to run for office is: why? This question will come from voters, friends, your family, and your opponent. You must have an answer that is simple, distinct, and makes sense. This is your platform and should be limited to about three key points that you can discuss, with intelligence, at any given point. Whatever you say or put out in the media or say openly from that point is what you have to stick with, but before you work on your platform, you should figure out why you want to run.

People run for office for a variety of reasons. Some people run because something has so angered them that they want to see a change, and some people just run because they want power. I ran for political office for several reasons. Primarily, I saw people who were running for office and thought to myself, *I can be that person.* We were seeing cuts due to the recession, and I thought I could make an impact to save money and help protect the community. It was a big—no, huge—risk for me financially. I only had two years left to fully retire and risked that and much more. I went in knowing nothing about the process and found little assistance because I was running against a strong third-term incumbent.

The local Supervisor of Elections Office was very good about giving basic assistance to a new candidate, but it was overwhelming, to say the least. Through a mutual friend, I was introduced to Ryan O'Reilly, who was a local firefighter-paramedic. Ryan had a political science degree and had actually run for a school board position in his hometown. The Ryan Doctrine, as we called it from the Tom Clancy *Jack Ryan* spy series, was where I learned most of the strategies for my first election. I lost that election by just a few percentage points, and it was very disappointing. I had never worked so hard at something in my life and had put $25,000 of my savings into it. The hardest part was the time I was not able to spend with my family, and even though it was less than a year, I put everything I could into that election. I will discuss many of the issues I had during this election throughout my book for you to understand the emotions that running for office can bring out. My wife was and still is the driving force in my life—I seriously considered dropping out of that first race several times, but she kept me going. I know she was not happy about me running the second time, but she never discouraged me from running, even though the odds were even tougher on the second run.

Whatever the reason you run, you must understand that there is a lot more to running for a political office than the proverbial "shaking hands and kissing babies." Whether it is your local homeowners association or a municipal, county, state, or federal public office, the decisions you make can potentially affect the lives of real people and have financial impacts in the billions of dollars. So back to the original question, why do people run for office?

## The World Changer

Many people who run for office start with the idea that they want to change the world, or at least their little part of it. I have seen people run for office because they wanted a traffic light put up, and I have seen people run for office to stop global warming. These candidates may be the most passionate about their campaign and may be more aggressive when running against, but they must realize there are a multitude of issues to consider. What happens if they take office and succeed in what they were running for? Do they quit? Sometimes the World Changer knows they have little chance of victory, but they want to make their statement in a public forum.

## The Avenger

The Avenger may go at the campaign with the same or even more zeal than the World Changer. This candidate is looking for revenge for a perceived wrong done to them or others. The Avenger may be running against an incumbent or running for an office within a system which they think wronged them. If you are running for this reason, remember politics are a "no gloves" fight, so be ready to defend all your actions, both now and in the past. Everything you have done in the past or present is open to the public and there is little sympathy for those running for office.

## The Public Servant

The hope is all people running for public office do so with a servant's heart. Running for any elected position takes effort and opens the candidate's life up for public viewing and scrutiny. Those who truly serve in the best interest of the community are those who run for positions that pay little or nothing and are not glamorous. Many of these positions are found serving particular boards and in small communities. Like the other positions, the candidate will be questioned as to their motive to run for office. Sometimes giving the answer that they are running to serve the community has been unfortunately used too many times by unscrupulous politicians, and the community has lost trust in them.

## *The Professional*

There are those who take on the world of political candidacy as a profession. This may be a childhood dream that expands into adult life, or it may be the elected official who builds their entire career on running for office and becoming re-elected. Whatever the case, this person looks at their position as you would look at the job you currently hold. This professional politician will protect their job and fight for it. Whatever their reason for running in the first place or continuing to run, this is that person's livelihood and they will defend it. This is very good to remember when you are running against an incumbent.

One of the ways I have explained this to people asking me about running against an incumbent whose primary occupation is politics is to consider how you would feel if someone were trying to take your job. Your job that supports you and your family is something you will fight for, and this is the same, whether you like it or not. I would never discourage someone from running against someone, but if it were merely to take their job away from them, then I might have to question that. Running for office needs to be for a reason, and if you are running against an incumbent or against others, you need to show why you are the better person for the job.

## Running for the Money

Many political offices pay little to no money at all. These are positions that are associated with various boards, associations, and small cities and counties. In some cases, political figures may be given a small stipend per month for reimbursement for travel or other expenses, but in other cases politicians may receive up to six figures annually with retirement and healthcare benefits. These higher paying positions are usually found in higher municipal, county, state, and federal government. I believe the thought process behind this was to ensure that those who take office devote the majority of time to their work. This amount subsidizes or replaces what they would make in their original career. As with the professional politicians, those who are in it for the money are going to fight very hard to keep their paychecks and benefits. You should keep this in mind when you are running against them.

One should fully consider the number of hours that are devoted to being in public office and whether it is economically feasible to do so. Besides meetings, which may only be scheduled a few times a month, one must also consider the public events which may take more time to prepare for than the event itself. You are now a public figure, and throwing on your favorite jeans, old t-shirt, and ball cap do not always work now. Having an ample supply of clean suits and business attire is a must, plus the upkeep takes time and money. Also figure in that workshops, one-on-one meetings with government staff, business leaders, and constituents cannot always be on your preferred time frame. The public expects accessibility to you. Finally, emails, phone calls, monitoring social media and the press also take significant portions of your time, and people expect quick responses to their questions and concerns. In all, it is not uncommon for even a small town elected official to put in thirty to sixty hours a week.

## *Running for the Power*

Winning an election is an adrenaline rush few have felt. Even in less glamorous elected positions, there is an aura of stardom or glamour. The title given to a position can be overwhelming itself, no matter what the position is. Once you see or hear your name with your office title, it changes your thought process, even if only slightly. People will treat you with a different type of respect even if you are the mayor of the town of only a few dozen people. You are now the representative of the community and you are seen in a different light than before.

Depending on the position and the location where you reside, most public officials cannot be removed unless they are voted out in the next election or removed by the governor or higher political authority. Many times you are the proverbial "buck stops here" when you talk to people. This can have its advantages and disadvantages, especially when speaking to voters. An advantage is that unlike corporate America, an elected official can make a decision that does not always work out successfully and in most cases, they cannot be removed immediately from office. Unlike the football coach who loses the big game or the CEO who did not meet quarterly sales, you keep your job, at least until the next election; the disadvantage is the same—until the next election. Every vote you cast and every decision you make can be held against you later. This is important to know for incumbents and those running against the incumbent—do research on yourself and your opponent.

## *The Stand-In*

This may be a person who is asked to run by a person or a group to fill an open spot or to run against an incumbent who the sponsors want replaced. There is nothing wrong with this concept, and it happens more than people know. Many people do not want to run for office for a variety of reasons but are able to support a candidate. These individuals or groups are important to identify if you are the opposition or if you are willing to run and need a backer.

As you will understand as you read this book, running for office and serving as an elected official puts you in a spotlight. Your life, both good and bad, are transparent, and there are very few restrictions on what people can say about you. In fact, I know of several people who were blatantly slandered during their run for office. They contacted attorneys and were told that the courts look at "mudslinging" during an election as a cost of doing business. We will go into depth about the vetting process and the positives and negatives in chapter 4.

If you are that person asked by a person or a group to run for a public office, I hope you are reading this book. There is so much more to being an elected official than just showing up for a meeting or two and making a vote that will probably coincide with that person's or group's beliefs. Hopefully, the beliefs of the sponsor are the same as yours.

*"That would be Cool"*

Running for office because it would be "cool" is actually a term I have heard a few times in my career. Maybe it is that proverbial bucket list thing to check off or some other reason, but some people enter elections solely for this reason. Many times the person doing this is young and may just meet the qualifications of age or other basic qualifications to run. I believe this is because as we grow older, we have more life experiences that we may not want to share with the world or don't want to take the chance. Even though I cannot think of someone who has actually won an election who has done this, I am sure there are some. Never take any opponent for granted. I have seen this happen far too many times where the favored candidate does not take an underdog candidate seriously and has lost. You never know—the person who is running against you because "it would be cool" may just have a cooler name or spot on the ballot that voters like. Take every opponent seriously!

There are probably a dozen other reasons why one may want to run for public office. Whatever the reason is, the one thing to remember is that you have to give it 100 percent—no, 110 percent—of your life while you are doing it. If you have put the most effort into something in your life, well, you need to put more into an election to win. To John Q. Public, an elected official may just be someone who shows up to cut ribbons and shake hands, but the fact is most public officials have an immense amount of power that can change the lives of people and change the nation, no matter how small of a position they have.

Whatever your reason is for running, remember, voters do not want to hear that you are running just because you thought it would be fun, or that you like to have power over other people, or definitely not because you want the money. You have to have a reason that appeals to voters and is easily explainable. Practice these reasons and always be ready for somebody to ask you the question: Why are you running?

# Chapter 2

# Can I Run for Office?

Believe it or not, there are very few prerequisites to running for public office. With the exception of some specific elected positions, such as judges and others, there are no educational requirements, no credit checks, and in most cases, no background check. In fact, throughout the United States there are elected officials making decisions on multimillion- to billion-dollar budget items—if these same people were in the corporate world, they may not even be qualified for an entry-level job, never mind be in management.

This has always been hard for me to understand, but I had to realize that an elected official is a representative of the public. Our system was built to have decisions made by people who represent the majority. You must check your local guidelines for the position you are running for to make sure you qualified. This is extremely important to do before filing to run or actually taking office. I have personally seen several people who were running find out they were not qualified due to technicalities, including residency requirements. Each type of election is different and each location has different rules. Many states differ in their requirements, and federal election laws are much different than local election laws.

The most common election requirements deal with minimum age, residency requirements, citizenship, and whether the candidate is a registered voter. Though there are few requirements to become a registered voter, the issue of being a convicted felon has been challenged in several states, and several of the states have allowed convicted felons to vote. In 2016, Florida passed a law allowing convicted felons to have the ability to vote but never clarified whether or not a convicted felon could run for office. This has become an issue in at least one local election in the state of Florida in which a candidate was elected for the seat of city council, and then it was brought out that he was a convicted felon. In the end, the city's charter stated that an elected official cannot be a convicted felon, and the council voted to have another election.

Besides the embarrassment this has surely caused the person running and the confusion within the city, elections are expensive, especially in larger elections. An election in an area of just 50,000 voters may cost up to or more than $100,000 each, depending on the area's requirements. In many areas elections officials, town clerks, or whoever is responsible for accepting and maintaining election paperwork does not give advice on how to run. They also do not make the interpretations of the law but merely accept the paperwork in which the candidate attests to the fact that he or she is qualified to run for office.

In many states throughout the country, the secretary of state is the chief elections officer and is responsible for elections. Some states, like Florida, have an elected supervisor of elections for each county who is responsible for elections. These positions are not nonpartisan, which means that the person running goes on the ballot under their chosen political party. There are no requirements to be elected to the office other than to meet the basic residency, age, voter eligibility, and non-convicted felon status. Technically, with most elected positions there are no prerequisites for knowledge of elections or experience working in the elections system in any form. The position is one of the most crucial elected positions in our country, in my opinion. This person is responsible for ensuring that our most sacred right of choosing our leaders is held to a standard that is not just fair, but legal.

In 2018, then Governor Rick Scott suspended the Broward County supervisor of elections for not following the law in that year's election. There are checks and balances with elections, and in my area, there is a canvassing board that carefully reviews certain ballots in an area accessible to the public view. This board consists of the supervisor of elections, a county court judge, and the chair of the county board of commissioners. These positions must be replaced by alternates if the person in that position is being opposed. I have the utmost confidence in the supervisor of elections in my area for his honesty, integrity, and experience. As a candidate, you need to review the laws—all the laws—involved in your campaign. Remember, it is you, not your campaign manager or anyone else, who signs that you meet the qualifications to run, and most times this document is under oath with the possibility of civil or criminal action for falsification. Ignorance of the law is no excuse, ever.

Most states have a requirement for petitions that signatures of registered voters need to be compiled and turned in to be qualified to run for office. Each state and each local government has differing rules on the number of petitions and dates that these petitions must be turned in. This is a very important factor that a candidate has to know all the information about. Many areas require that a percentage of the registered voters sign a petition for the candidate to officially be on the ballot. This is usually about one or two percent, which in a small area is not that many, but in an area that has over 100,000-plus registered voters, getting 1,000 petitions can be a daunting task.

The petitions must be verified by the elections official and may require signature verifications from the voters' original registration. In other words, you just don't go to the ball field or your local grocery store and have people sign a list. The forms are usually standardized with requirements on copying them. The information provided on the form must list specifics about the person signing it, and in some cases the person signing must personally fill out their full name, address, and date of birth. Some states allow the candidate to pay an amount in lieu of the petitions, but this is sometimes very costly and many times can be looked upon as negative because the candidate does not do the work to get the petitions or is thought not to have support. People are many times less willing to sign something when they must provide all their information.

As mentioned, obtaining petitions to get on a ballot requires a lot more when there are thousands required, and some state government positions may require hundreds of thousands of petitions for the person to get on the ballot. This necessitates either a large team of persons getting the petitions or a large fee to be paid, depending on the regulations. Some candidates elect to use professional petition collectors, who charge the candidate or campaign per verified petition. It is not uncommon for a professional petition gatherer to charge $1 to $2 or more per verified petition. If this is allowed in your area, make sure that you check all the rules and regulations and reporting requirements. Many areas will require you to report fees paid to individuals for petitions; remember to follow the federal IRS guidelines and reference 1099 forms where required. The last thing you want is to have a complaint filed either during your election or after it, showing that you have violated state, local or federal rules or laws.

If you do plan to obtain your own petitions, the best place to start is with friends and family. Make sure that the petitions are completely filled out and signed in the appropriate areas. If there is a form provided by your own local elections office or other official office, make sure that the form is copied correctly and, if allowed, highlight areas that people need to fill out. If you or your team are collecting petitions, always look for areas where there will be a large number of registered voters. Keep in mind that some areas, private businesses, or events will not allow you to collect petitions. This is their right since it is private property. Some public buildings may allow you to collect petitions, like the library or different government offices, but they may only allow you to do so in certain areas. Civic organizations, clubs, and political party meetings are also a good place to collect petitions—people understand the purpose and are willing to fill them out.

Use caution when having petitions filled out by people who are currently working because this may violate some of their work rules. There is no need to get someone in trouble or bring negative light to your campaign, especially in the early stages. Additionally, some nonprofit organizations may not be allowed to engage in political activities, and this could be considered a political activity that could cause the organization issues with their nonprofit status. It is always best to ask the manager or owner of any business, organization, or meeting prior to sending out petitions to ensure you do not harm them or cause yourself any problems. This may be your first and only contact with the voter—be professional and make sure anyone helping you is also professional while they represent you.

As stated earlier, residency issues are probably the most common reason that candidates get disqualified or have their victory challenged. Each election and each area has different rules pertaining to where a candidate must reside and when. Some areas only require the candidate to move into the district they are running for after they win, but some require the candidate to live in the district when they file. These roles are very strict and can cause a candidate to be disqualified or to possibly be removed after they win.

Do not expect your opponent to notify you or the elections officials that you are violating any of these rules during the election. Opposing candidates may wait until the outcome of the election to make a complaint. The reasons for waiting may include not wanting to file a complaint to open up an aggressive campaign or to simply see if the other candidate wins and then challenge the win. This may occur when the opposition is stronger and the candidate knows or feels that he or she will lose. They will keep these violations concealed until the outcome of the race so there are no additional challengers to them or so that they will win by default. In one case, I saw a candidate shrewdly let the election go up to a few days before the close of filing, which did not allow for anyone else to file to run, and then filed a complaint that the opposing candidate did not live in the district as required. The opposing candidate did not fully read the requirements and thought she could move into the district if she won. She had no other choice but to withdraw from the race. The outcome and appointment all depends on the elections district or area and their individual roles. Again, it is your responsibility to know the rules and again, do your opposition research to see if your opposition is in violation. If your opposition is in violation, weigh out your choices as to what is the best benefit for your campaign.

It is your responsibility as a candidate to ensure that you meet the qualifications. In many areas the elections official simply accepts and files paperwork. The elections official is, in many cases, not responsible for doing background checks or making sure that the information on the signed paperwork is correct. Additionally, many times election forms are official documents that require the candidate swear to their signature with an oath of truthfulness, which could lead to perjury or other charges if the paperwork is falsified. Consult your local elections rules and regulations before signing or filing any paperwork. This information is usually provided to you or you can easily find it with an internet search.

In many areas write-in candidates are allowed on the ballot. This is where a voter can write in the name of a person who does not have their name officially printed on the ballot. The chance of winning an election by write-in is very slim, but there are some. Some areas still require the write-in candidate to file paperwork prior to the election, or the write-in name is not accepted. These candidates who do file the proper paperwork are sometimes referred to as certified candidates and could potentially win if they receive enough votes. Depending on the area, a person who enters a race as a write-in may not need the required petitions to get on the ballot. Again, rules on write-ins vary with every election and should be fully understood before filing. Write-in candidates can also be used to keep an election closed in certain circumstances, but for now Mickey Mouse, Elvis, and Krusty have yet to be put in the White House.

# Chapter 3

# What Office are You Running For?

With over 150,000 different offices to run for in the United States, there are many choices on how to serve. Hopefully, you already have in mind what office you want to run for. Like any job—and it is a job whether you get paid or not—you should research everything about it and learn more. There is a newer website called runforoffice.org that allows people to enter the area they live in and find out what elected positions there are. The site also gives basic descriptions of the elected positions and offers assistance through the process. This is a good start, but if you want to find out more about what is in your area, contact or search your Secretary of State site or the Supervisor of Elections Office website. Many meetings are aired on television or on the internet. YouTube is a good source of many government meetings and allows you to watch them at your leisure. If you are watching one of these meetings and it is extremely boring or makes no sense to you, then you probably need to research the position more. Agendas and full copies of the meetings can many times be found online and can be hundreds of pages long. It is a good insight to what the job entails when you read the agenda and watch the meeting. Most people have no idea what a mayor, city council member, county commissioner, or school board member does, but you need to know if you plan on running.

I don't think there is any American who has not dreamt of being the president of the United States at one time or another. Since there have been fewer than fifty presidents in the history of the United States, the odds of a person being president is incredibly slim. Obviously, the run for president is the ultimate election process in the United States and the most costly. With estimates of the 2016 presidential election costing over $2 billion dollars, a serious run for the White House is out of reach for the majority of Americans. This does not mean you cannot run for president—every four years there are many people who put in their names to win the highest office in the land. The subject of being president and presidential campaigns could be a volume of books in itself, so for that reason we will leave this campaign to our future novels.

On the federal level there are other positions including Congress or the House of Representatives and the US Senate. Depending on the population of a state, there are more congressmen than there are senators, with the exception of seven states that only have one congressional member who represents the entire state. Each state has two senators, and there are varying numbers of congressmen with over fifty congressional seats in the state of California. Obviously, the senate race is much more difficult than a congressional race in at least forty-three states, and it's more costly. Senate races have cost well over $100 million in several races. Though congressional races have not reached the $100 million mark yet, there are many that have run in the tens of millions of dollars. A lot of money for a job that pays $174,000 a year, and no, that is not a lifetime salary. The federal elections commission has information on running for all federal positions and should definitely be reviewed prior to any thought of running for these positions.

State-level elected positions vary widely with each individual state. Each state has a governor, and in some areas the lieutenant governor is also separately elected. Various other positions, some of which mirror those of the federal government, are elected positions throughout the state, including a state house of representatives and a state senate. These positions are easier to obtain than a federal position but are also very contentious at times and very expensive. The pay for many of these state positions is lower than that of even a county position in some areas, but there are reimbursements for other expenses that add to the job. Research these jobs extensively because many may require you to relocate or stay for long periods of time in your state capitol during session.

Counties, parishes, and boroughs have various elected positions, which include commissioners, sheriffs, judges, and a variety of other positions that are up for election and varying terms. These positions may or may not be paying positions depending on what they are, but most do receive a paycheck or some type of stipend. Some of the positions are paid based upon the number of citizens living in the particular area. School boards also fall under individual counties in most states, and some counties have an elected superintendent of schools, but this position has been dwindling away over the years to be replaced with a superintendent who is hired by the school board. Additionally, there may be other positions including district boards or other positions that may require an election of voters to be seated.

Municipalities or cities also have similar positions as counties. They also vary from city to city and state to state. The function of these elected positions also vary from city to city even if they are in the same county. The mayor may sit on a council and be a voting member, while in the same county a different city mayor may not be allowed to vote and is only there as a figurehead. Each city also has a different role as to who runs the elections—this may be the city clerk, who may contract out to an elections official either with the county or the state to conduct their official elections.

Research what position you want to run for prior to doing so. Find out whether or not there are any rules that forbid you from taking a position such as a dual office requirement. This restricts persons from being in two elected positions at one time, but it can also restrict people holding certain positions from being elected officials. An example of this is the state of Florida, which does not allow a person to hold two offices at one time. This is a restriction that also does not allow certified law enforcement officers to hold public office. In Florida, a sworn law enforcement officer who has arrest abilities cannot be an elected official, even if they do not work in the area in which they are an elected official. In general, I understand this concept that a person who has arrest powers in the same area they are an elected official may run into conflicts of interest, especially if the law enforcement officer's elected position gives them the power to vote on ordinances. An elected official who is a sworn law enforcement officer in Florida cannot even work, reserve, or volunteer in any jurisdiction in the entire state, even if they have no say in that community's budgeting or law-making process.

I was a reserve deputy sheriff, bomb technician, and SWAT-medic prior to getting elected and volunteered countless hours. I inactivated my certificate and continue to teach at our local police academy and volunteer at the fire department, but I was unable to go to another city or county to volunteer to fill in as a school resource officer after the state mandated security in schools following a large school shooting. I also personally know of several well-qualified individuals who would make wonderful elected officials who did not want to give up their careers or weren't allowed to volunteer their time as law enforcement officers due to this law, including one who was already in office and had to also inactivate his certification. The dual office restriction is part of the Florida Constitution and could not be easily changed and would most likely only be challenged if someone took office and tried to do both. Somewhere in the history of Florida, there may have been a police chief who was elected mayor, which I'm sure would have made for interesting town hall meetings. I am not sure of the background, but for now this is a great example of researching your position.

Specific municipal, city, and town charters along with other county ordinances and other similar items may also restrict those who can hold office. These restrictions many times restrict city or county employees from taking office if they are currently employed in and have other restrictions; for instance, the person cannot be a convicted felon. These rules, especially when it comes to residency requirements, need to be looked at prior to running to make sure there are no issues.

Again, look at the pay and benefits, if there are any. As mentioned earlier, some positions may pay nothing and some may pay a regular salary with insurance and retirement benefits. Also, do not expect it to be a simple task to look up the position you want. Yes, an internet search is a good start, but just finding the name of the position you want can sometimes be challenging. For example, according to the National Association of Counties, the majority of states use the term "county commissioner" as the elected official in county governments that vote on decisions related to the administration of general government duties. As we have been finding, each state has differences as to how these elected officials are referred to. Nine states refer to this position as a supervisor and in Florida, there is at least one very large Community Development District, or CDD, that calls their municipal elected leaders supervisors. Six states use councilor, two use justice of the peace, Alaska uses mayor, New Jersey uses freeholder, Louisiana uses police jurors, and in addition to justice of the peace, Kentucky also uses judge. So keep this in mind when you are looking at positions to run for and if you are moving from state to state.

Potential voters will ask you what the position you are

running for does. This will come along with the question of why you are running. Expect these questions and be ready to answer them during the election and after you win. A good resource to ready yourself is the National League of Cities and the National Association of Counties. Both of these websites have descriptions of the positions for some areas of county and city government. They are a good start and help you to learn information that your opponents may not know, even the incumbents.

# Chapter 4

# Vetting

Vetting is the thorough investigation of a candidate either prior to or during the election. Another thing you should do before you consider filing to run for an election is a thorough self-vetting. The best suggestion that I could ever give anybody on this subject is: do not think someone will not find out something you are trying to hide. No one knows you better than yourself, but in this day and age of cameras, public records, and social media, it is easy to find information on anybody. You will also have to file a financial affidavit at some point listing all debts and assets. These forms are public record and are signed legal documents.

If you hire a professional campaign manager or consultant, one of the first things they will do is to meet with you and ask you what you have to hide. Do not take this offensively, and if they are not asking that, they are not doing their job properly. In fact, they should have already done a background check on you or had their staff do it. You should be completely honest with them and not hide any information because if you do and it comes out later in an election, they will be the person to stand by you and to help you get through it. One suggestion is to have the potential campaign manager or consultant sign a nondisclosure agreement before hiring them to ensure that if you part ways at a later time, they cannot hold the information you told them against you or give it to your opposition. I hate even hearing this phrase and hate even more writing it, but my best suggestion in reference to these types of contracts to protect yourself is to consult an attorney to make sure the contract is legal. I know not everyone can afford a $450 an hour or more attorney, but this is important, and if you are going through the expense of doing this, get a general contract for those who are working with you so they do not leak strategy. I am not saying have your mom sign a waiver before holding a sign for you, just make sure your key staff, mostly a paid consultant or manager, does not go and help the other side. The consultant I use has this built into his contract, and I know he is reputable. I know this because he ran my opposition's campaign in the last election as well as several others I had been involved with over the years and I saw his integrity.

Your campaign manager will not be the only person who wants to do a full vetting of you. Contributors and supporters will also ask you the same questions or will have background checks completed. Though some background companies do not allow users to access their data base to do research on political candidates, some private investigators will still do backgrounds after being hired by a potential contributor or supporter. I was surprised when I went to meet a contributor who had a complete file on my entire life history. The information the contributor had even included my credit score and other financial information, which in the long run saved me time in running all that myself. I knew there was nothing out there to find that was not already public record, so I had not made running financial information a priority.

Opposition research is not new and has been around probably since the first caveman ran against another caveman for head of the cave. Well, they probably just fought it out with clubs, but you get the idea. There are books and even seminars on how to conduct this research into your opposition. In large elections this research is usually run through a law firm, but on the streets it is a private investigator or legal assistant doing the research. These professional researchers are not limited to just the big elections—an internet search will reveal dozens of private investigators and firms willing to do opposition research for a price, and it can be expensive. A good investigator will probably start around $75 an hour, in addition to the costs and markup for running backgrounds. Sometimes this information will be good, and sometimes you will find out that your opponent has nothing, which may still be good if you have some shady areas that you do not want out.

If you do not have the resources to pay an investigator, which you should technically claim as a political expense, or you have a bad feeling about all the "spy stuff," you or even a friend can do the opposition research yourself. I still suggest it not be you as the candidate, and always remember internet provider (IP) addresses can always be traced and lead right back to you. As I mentioned before, I was a law enforcement officer prior to becoming an elected official. I had a variety of assignments as an investigator and spent a large portion of my career as a drug agent and supervisor for a multi-agency drug, vice, and at times everything else type unit. This means we would assist with other crimes needing detectives and undercover personnel. One of the things I learned being an investigator was that public records were one of the best sources of information there was. I found that public records give more in-depth detail and are either obtainable via the internet or by going to the records custodian or courthouse of the area where the person lived. This may take some traveling if the person has lived in different locations, but the information is more detailed than an electronic background check. Now, you could pay a private investigator to go and do this hands-on research if you wish, but just remember the costs. One disadvantage of doing the research yourself is that many times you may be recognized as the person looking into your opposition. This may put your opponent immediately on the defensive, even if they have nothing to hide. They may start the same type of research on you or prepare for an aggressive or "dirty mudslinging" campaign. Many states have public records laws which do not require the requestor to identify themselves to look up records or even obtain copies. There is usually a charge for printed copies for extensive research, and this may be paid in cash. Just remember, there are eyes everywhere and it could make it back to your opponent that somebody is looking into their background.

As stated earlier, self-vetting should be your first step in the campaign process. This should probably be done somewhere between the area of figuring out why you want to run and part of the "can I run" process. A lot of times you can change the legal requirements, with the exception of age and where you were born, but you cannot change those things that may embarrass you from your past. The phrase I always use is, "I don't want to do anything bad that my kids would see on the front page of the newspaper." That is kind of an outdated saying because most likely something bad would be posted on social media within seconds, and I cannot say when the last time the children have actually purchased the paper version of our local newspaper. The point is, I do not want to embarrass my family and neither should you. If you have something in your past, especially something that your family doesn't know about or you don't want them to know about, then either tell them before giving any further thought or consideration to whether you really want to run for office. Over the years, elected officials have been stereotyped as liars, cheats, and on the take. This is usually the uninformed public response to an unpopular decision. With that in mind, people are already looking at you when you run for office. Do not think that there is anything you can hide, since your entire life will now be under a microscope. I know people who bank photos and information away for future use. You never know when it may come out.

Below are several suggestions for you to do your own self-vetting, and I suggest you to use it as a type of checklist to consider:

Affairs: Unfortunately affairs are commonplace in American society and are probably one of the main destroying factors in any political campaign. Look back at your life and consider if there are any of these issues that are public and have been brought out or if they are private but have not been discovered. As you notice, I use the wording "have not been discovered." Once you become a public figure and more people see that you are running for office, things change drastically. Someone from your past may never have wanted to broadcast any of this information, but when you become a public figure, there are many different motivations that drive people to attempt to expose you. Those whom you unconditionally trust may turn on you for whatever reason. Do not dismiss the fact that you may be followed during an election. I cannot stress enough that elections are very serious, and there are many things you have no clue about that are riding on the outcome. It may not only be your opposition who may follow you, but also supporters of your opposition, the press, or someone who just does not like you for whatever reason. There are also freelance investigators who may be actual private investigators or someone who wants to get their fifteen minutes of fame by discovering something on anyone. You are marketing yourself and your name, which leaves you open in every aspect.

Arrests and run-ins with the law: If you have ever been arrested or had a run-in with law enforcement and it was negative, it will most likely come out in your election. Even if you have had the case sealed, the information may come out. It is not uncommon to have opposition research include contacting all those involved in a case, even if the candidate was a victim or just a witness. Be prepared to address these issues at any time.

Marriages and domestic issues: Your marriage or marriages will definitely be a large part of your election. For people to say that family is off limits in an election is merely wishful thinking. Even if candidates signed a non-aggression pact with each other, this does not mean that supporters or political action committees cannot put out negative information about you or your family. There is nobody who can give more dirt on a person than spouses or a significant other.

Be prepared for these types of questions and prepare your family. My father, who was eighty-six at the time, was called and told that I would be "ruined" if I ran for office. My mom had just passed away the year before and it upset him. I strongly believe my opponent had nothing to do with this call and it was a rogue supporter, but nevertheless, it was a lesson on the negative side. After this, my dad became one of my biggest supporters and went door to door for me getting petitions and handing out palm cards. Previously, he was not active due to seeing the ups and downs my mom went through in the decades of working in local political campaigns, but up until he died in late 2018, he was a constant sight and will be missed by all. He and my mother were proudly laid to rest in Arlington National Cemetery for his military service during World War II and Korea. He was a kamikaze survivor and Purple Heart recipient. I would not be the person I am now without their strong influences.

Finances: Though there is no requirement for good credit or to have no financial problems, your finances, good or bad, can come up. Your finances will be scrutinized, and remember that bankruptcies and financial judgments are public record. Lawsuits and other information can easily be obtained or from others involved. Even a person you have had bad financial dealings with or believes you have wronged them can come out against you. Do not think that a person who you owe money to or who has been involved with you or your business will not find the opportunity to get revenge at an open public meeting. You are the most vulnerable while you are running for office and in the public eye.

The thought that if you are rich, you are a good businessperson and if you are poor, you are irresponsible does not always have the same impact it used to. With the recession in the late 2000s through early 2010s, people had a different outlook on both the financially challenged and the wealthy. Many wealthy people were looked at as privileged and many of the financially challenged were looked at as victims of greed from large corporations and other entities. Though gender, race, and other areas used to define discrimination should never be a part of politics, a word of caution would be to fully analyze using one's finances against an opponent. In one political race that I was told about, a male candidate used his female opponent's past bankruptcy against her as a point that she would not be financially responsible to handle the position she was running for; she countered that her husband had cheated on her, left her, and she had to raise her son on her own. It could have easily gone either way, and I do not know the complete details of the event or the candidate, but the use of one's finances can be very delicate and bring out emotions on all sides.

Think ahead when it comes to using finances, or anything for that matter, in opposition to your opponent. Rehearse and debate everything in your head. I found the best time for doing this was driving to or between events. It will usually not be your opponent who brings something up, but a person in the crowd who may or may not have been staged to ask the question. Think of every question you will ask or even subtly mention about your opponent. Using the above scenario about the female candidate answering that her husband left her, do you then find out if she gets alimony and child support and how much, or do you just leave it alone? Thoughts when you are questioning a person's finances are if they have sick family members, were they a victim of crime, or was there a death in the family that hurt them. Be careful, but be ready for anything.

Political Affiliations: Organizations that you belong to or that you have belonged to in the past, especially if they are controversial, will always come up during an election. The political parties that you belonged to are public record and may make a difference, even in a non-partisan race. Look back at all the organizations you have belonged to and any of their ties to opposing political parties, and be ready to defend yourself if needed. What may seem to be a simple or longtime past meeting or membership may come back to haunt you. Think about meetings you have attended and those impromptu photos that you get pulled into with other candidates or people you do not know. Someone gets a photo of you posing with or just talking to a controversial person and then it is posted all over social media in a negative light. Most of the time you don't want to be rude or have no idea the photo was taken, but go through the websites and social media of the meetings, fundraisers, dinners and other events you have been to and see if you picture is there. Remember, once you become a candidate, people will scroll through their pictures to see if you were there, and it can show up at any place and at any time.

You should also review your political contributions in the past, if you have any. Be prepared to defend these contributions, which are always public record. This includes federal, state and local politics. Sometimes when people go to fundraisers for what they may just think of as a party and pay for a ticket, they are actually listed as contributors to a political campaign. A search of the records for political campaigns and every area you have lived in should be done to ensure that you have all the information needed. If you have access to old checkbooks or accounts, review these for any contributions or areas that may be questionable. Your opposition will definitely search your name, but so will supporters on both sides, the media, and voters will also look you up. Never try to hide anything and definitely never try to have something removed that was public record. It always amazes me the ignorance of some people who try to remove information that is public record or already recorded. There is always an imprint of everything in today's digital environment. Be prepared and be transparent. It's hard for people to fight a truthful answer. Many times just saying, "I am telling you the truth, and I don't know what else I can do" stops the accuser in their tracks. The worst outcome is for you to get obviously flustered or try to deny an accusation. This is a win to your opposition.

Medical Issues: Most people believe that HIPAA laws protect you as a candidate as well as your family members against the discovery or the use of medical conditions during an election. Technically they do, but as with everything else, information seems to have a way of leaking out. Health problems may not be an issue during an election, but do not be surprised if a health problem is not seen as a weakness. This would also include family members who have health issues because it may be thought that you would not be able to devote enough time to the office if you are taking care of a sick relative. Elections and politics are not fair.

Take care of yourself physically. I have had physically demanding jobs my entire life, but nothing has taken a toll on me like running for public office. You always need to be smiling and appear in a good mood. Shake hands and greet everyone you meet and say your name, even if you are not introducing yourself as a candidate. Hide sanitizer or better yet, sanitizer wipes in your pockets or purse. Don't use them in view of people after you shake their hand, which I have seen someone do. No better way to subliminally tell someone you do not want to touch them than using sanitizing hand gel immediately after shaking their hand, even if it is true.

Social Media: Social media has changed the way Americans vote and may have possibly changed the outcome of elections as seen in the 2016 American election cycle. Though social media is one of the best tools to get your name out, it can also be the destruction of a political campaign. As a prospective candidate or manager of a campaign, one must immediately evaluate their own social media accounts. A full review of all pictures, comments, and even pages that are liked or shared should be done with the understanding that anyone may have seen them and copied the pages. Just because you delete the information does not mean that it cannot be retrieved or that someone else has not taken a screen shot of it or saved it in the past.

Personal messaging and other forms of communication via social media should also be scrutinized. You should take a self-account of everything you have texted or messaged to other people including family members. Messages and private pictures always have a way of turning up during elections, and they should be reviewed carefully. Many a candidate or already elected official have had their political career ended by nude photos or offensive photos such as offensive Halloween costumes or college sorority or fraternity photos. This will be the easiest area to scrutinize you personally, and your opponent will follow you online or have others do so. The vast number of social media and electronic venues is vast and have changed tremendously over the past couple decades. Dating sites and other similar sites are also easily accessed and should be carefully considered along with all other types of social media.

The vetting process for any candidate cannot be overlooked. An honest account of one's past must be done to avoid embarrassment not only to the candidate, but their family, friends and contributors. It starts with the self-vetting process and continues with the campaign manager or consultant. The more a person has been vetted, the better the chance that no unexpected issues will come up.

# Chapter 5

# Money, Money, and More Money

No matter what type of campaign you want to run, there is a monetary cost. Even if it is a small local campaign in which the candidate simply goes and talks to each voter, it still takes time, and all time has a monetary value. Unfortunately, the majority of campaigns do not rely simply on a candidate going and talking to every voter personally to win his or her vote. The printing of materials, including petitions, paperwork, and filing fees are just a start. Some areas require a political bank account and also require filing fees or fees for processing petitions and other paperwork. These fees may be paid by the candidate directly or can come out of the campaign account. Either way, there are costs associated with a political campaign.

A term that is heard in many campaigns is "grassroots campaign." A grassroots campaign is basically one that does not spend a large amount of money and uses word of mouth or other inexpensive ways of spreading the word during an election. These are usually candidates who do not have contributors or funds of their own. Grassroots campaigns have a hard time competing with larger campaigns that are well funded due to the fact that marketing costs can be very high.

It is a misconception of many people that campaign signs, buttons, and other forms of advertisement do not cost anything. These items are not cheap and take a large amount of funds to produce. Mailers, which will be discussed in depth in chapter 10, are one of the most expensive areas in any campaign. With each mailer costing anywhere from fifty cents to two dollars or more, the costs add up quickly. For this reason, candidates rely heavily on contributors to support their campaign. Candidates must know election laws, which will be discussed in the next chapter, and be cautious of amounts and contributors from certain organizations. Some organizations are not allowed to contribute to political campaigns due to their nonprofit status, which does not allow them to be involved in political campaigns.

The best way to determine how much a campaign will cost is to look at the financial records for similar campaigns in the past. The amount spent in not only the position you are running for, but other positions within the same area should be considered carefully. If the past race was highly contested, the amount collected by both sides should be added together as a good gauge of where you may need to be for your election. It is not uncommon for local races bidding for the positions of city council, commissioner, or sheriff to exceed several hundred-thousand dollars. If you do not have a base of contributors, you can look to past contributors or people who have contributed to similar positions and seek them out for your election. Of course, you will look to friends and family for help first, but start by thinking to yourself, "Why would I contribute to this campaign?" What people would have an interest in you obtaining that position or would want to see you in there? People just do not give you money if they do not know you or know what your plans are.

As mentioned in a previous chapter, social media has changed the field of political campaigns. Several social media platforms, including Facebook, are now regulating political pages and maybe restricting them in the future. According to the Facebook website and multiple pages and links to find the information, it appears that currently, political pages will need to be approved and will require a screening process. This process requires the account information be submitted on a computer rather than those untraceable burner phones, and in the United States, specific forms of government identification must be submitted. The disclaimer line must also appear stating it is a political advertisement with the "Paid for by" statement. Even though these rules are in place, I have seen several people using their personal Facebook profiles for political purposes. Social media is still a good way to get your name marketed and one of the least costly forms of advertising.

Many political advisers will tell you not to turn down any money at any time. I have not always followed their advice on this subject, but this is an issue you as the candidate will have to handle personally. There may be some businesses or groups that you will obviously not want to have in your public financial records, but this depends on the demographics in your electoral district. The same goes for individuals who may have undesirable criminal records or belong to controversial or subversive groups—do you really want them to show up on your contribution list? I have also heard candidates telling people that a contribution is a tax write-off. You should consult with your tax professional, but in most cases contributions to a political campaign cannot be deducted from any personal or business taxes.

Contributions to a political campaign are public record. Many people and businesses will hesitate  contributing to a political campaign, especially when there is an incumbent, out of fear of retaliation if the person they contributed to loses. Political events in which money is collected must be reported and the names of those contributing must be recorded. As stated above, you should use caution in taking contributions from various people or groups that could hurt your campaign by association. It is hard to control the intake of funds, especially if you are selling tickets to an event. I am not suggesting having a background run on every person who comes to a fundraising event, but at least review the list before it is published and if need be, return the funds with the proper documentation. Additionally, your opponent may have someone contribute a small amount to your campaign to hurt you, or another candidate for another race may give you a small amount to try to link your campaigns as if they were supporting you. This may be to get your supporters to vote for them, thinking that the two of you are working together. Remember, politics can be nasty!

Soliciting political contributions is one of the most difficult parts of any campaign and should be done early to build a so-called war chest to both intimidate opponents and to show support. In addition to the large contributions, it is also a good practice to have large numbers of smaller contributions that show support from individuals. Many areas also regulate the taking of cash and how to handle anonymous contributions.

I would venture to say that no political candidate likes soliciting contributions during a campaign. Sometimes a candidate will find those who are able to solicit for them, but these people must also be aware of the campaign finance regulations and laws to avoid any errors. As will be discussed in the next chapter, the handling of finances should be carefully maintained. Most campaigns require the appointment of a treasurer, who can be a separate person or the candidate themselves. It is highly suggested that any treasurer be very familiar with the campaign laws and be trusted to handle the collection and spending of money in a timely manner. Some political advisers suggest the treasurer be a highly regarded businessperson for name purposes only, but this can backfire during the campaign if that treasurer is disliked by others. Use caution when assigning a treasurer, especially with one who is not familiar with campaign financing.

Additionally, banks may not be familiar with opening campaign accounts, and one should be very careful to ensure that the proper paperwork is completed and the account is named properly. Intermingling of funds will cause serious problems and may result in campaign violations and possible criminal charges. The banking industry has made the process of managing accounts very convenient recently. One can go on their mobile device and check all their accounts and even transfer money with a couple entries and swipes. If your campaign account is linked to the same banking portal as your personal and business accounts, use caution that those with access to the accounts do not accidently transfer funds to or from the campaign account that are not allowed, or if they are allowed, that they are properly reported. My suggestion is to set up a standalone account or use a separate bank completely just to keep the process transparent and to avoid errors. Always consult your local elections officials or rules for questions on campaign finance.

# Chapter 6

# Campaign Laws

Election laws differ in each type of election, whether it be state, federal, or local and with each state. Furthermore, individual districts, counties, municipalities and other areas all have differing rules and regulations. Just looking at the individual contribution limits from state to state will make your head spin. Some states only allow contributions to individuals of a few hundred dollars, whereas several states have unlimited individual contributions. As stated in the previous chapter, finances play a big part in any campaign, but there are also many laws and regulations to consider. There are multiple regulations and laws dealing with every election from local and state to federal, and these regulations and laws are regulated by several different officials. Violations of election regulations and laws can result in fines, removal, and even criminal charges. In many cases the elections officials merely process paperwork and do not do background checks or other investigations into wrongdoing. Ethics commissions and electoral commissions are usually those that evaluate any complaints and issue judgment as to any wrongdoing. In most cases, fines are issued to those who violate election regulations and laws unless there is obvious criminal wrongdoing.

Finances are the most regulated of election laws. In many areas, maximum amounts of contributions are strictly enforced. The way contributions are submitted, including timelines and proper reporting, are also regulated strictly. Timely reporting, which may include public reports throughout the campaign, are the responsibility of the candidate and the treasurer. Additionally, regulations on political action committees and other types of organizations are also strictly regulated. These political organizations have restrictions on what type of advertisements can be done and sometimes when information can be sent out.

As seen in the last decade, political disclaimers are very prevalent on media advertising. These disclaimers usually list the name of the candidate or the political organization placing the advertisement and many times state that the candidate or organization approves of the campaign. Some candidates have even used this requirement to get their point across that they "do approve of the message", or it has been used to bring a lighter comical side to the advertisement. Depending on the area and type of campaign, there is different wording, which may include the candidate's name, position they are running for, and the political party of the candidate, if applicable. These disclaimers are usually required for all media and physical advertising including mailers, signs, and literature from the campaign. Some areas do not require this disclaimer on small items such as trinkets or t-shirts, but it is always safe to put it on any item if possible. Candidates should always consult their local policies regarding how to word the disclaimer and what items are they required to be on. Remember, most of the time it comes to an interpretation of the law after a complaint, so document or keep items that have specific wording if needed in the future.

Many areas have regulations and ordinances on when signs and advertisements may be publicly placed and when they must be removed. The placing of signs should follow all regulations, including state and local traffic laws and reference to right-of-way violations. Many times enthusiastic supporters will line the roadways with small yard signs, which eventually are picked up and thrown away by code enforcement or other personnel. There are also regulations regarding the placement of signs on public property, and some states have special laws on the destruction of political signs. You should consult not only your local elections official, but your state laws and local county ordinances and city ordinances for any rules regarding the placement of signs.

If you see your opponent's sign and they are in violation, do not remove or even move the sign yourself. Let the officials in the area handle it through the proper channels or give your opponent a call or send him or her a message that they are placed wrongly. If they are rude to you, call the proper authorities about the sign or let someone else do it. This last thing you need is someone taking a picture of you pulling your opponent's sign out of the ground. Check with your local governing officials as to who is responsible for enforcement of wrongly placed signs or removing signs in violation. One of the governing areas I am acquainted with will dispose of signs in a clean dumpster and allow candidates or their workers to retrieve the signs. Just make sure you have permission to do so before attempting this. A trespass arrest probably will not look good for your campaign.

Campaigning and interfering in the voting process are also strictly regulated in all elections. Though the specifics are different for each area, distances for those holding signs and speaking to voters when entering polling places is regulated along with certain areas that campaigning cannot occur. Some candidates have purposely had supporters go into polling areas to vote with their campaign shirts on to get their names in front of the voters while they were entering their vote. When poll workers requested the voters with the campaign shirts on to cover them or even to turn them inside out, the wearers accused the poll workers of violating their First Amendment rights to free speech. As a person who constantly thinks of ways to market my name, I applaud their creativity, but also know that the negative scene a person can cause by wearing my name may lose many more voters than I could have ever gained.

Several areas require complaints to come from a verified source. These verified sources are provided to the candidate along with the complaint in a certain number of days. This eliminates anonymous complaints against candidates and also lessens the number of false accusations against candidates. Depending on the severity of the complaint, most are ruled on after elections and receive a monetary fine.

Campaign regulations and laws must be fully understood by candidates and their campaign members to avoid embarrassment and the possibility of violations that may risk the candidate from being elected or possibly being removed once in office. The best way for a candidate to ensure that he or she is not violating any regulations or laws is to review the information themselves and to have an experienced staff to assist. Experience is the best asset for any campaign when it comes to campaign and election laws, and hopefully this book is giving you direction to make your campaign successful and complaint-free.

# Chapter 7

# Getting Started

Now that you, the potential candidate, have self-vetted yourself, reviewed all the campaign regulations and laws, and decided what office to run for, it is now time to get started. You are going to become a public figure in a way that you never realized. All that you do will be noticed by not only those who may oppose you, but those who support you. You are running for a professional position which may be completely new to you.

Before getting out on the campaign trail, you should think of a slogan that you could use for speeches and to be put on your materials. Something short, memorable, and catchy is always best. Some memorable slogans include: I Like Ike, Putting People First, It's Time for Change, and Make America Great Again. If you cannot come up with an original slogan yourself, you can do a simple internet search to find a list of slogans that are applicable for each type of election.

In addition to a catchy slogan, you should also come up with at least three main stances for your campaign. These are the three additional things that you intend to do when you become elected. They need to be short, make sense for the position you are running for, and be easily memorized and explained by you. Once you have committed to these stances, you need to stick with them. You need to be able to easily discuss these areas and back up information if challenged. These will go on all your printed materials and be what you stand for. Some of the most popular stances include: lower taxes, cut waste, improve schools, increase jobs, and build a brighter future. If you pick any of these, you must be able to explain them in a manner in which you can first of all accomplish, plus be able to do in that position you are running for. If you are running for the mayor of the city and say that you are going to improve schools, that may be a great thought, but the school board may be the one who actually has control over public schools. Think about what your stances are and make sure that you follow them.

Put together a campaign committee. If you have chosen to use a professional campaign manager or adviser, have him or her vet this group and pick representatives that you both trust and respect. These will be the people whom you will depend on to help build your campaign. Pick people who will both support you and know your personality. This is also a way to bring on supporters, but just keep in mind that they are there to help build your campaign, and you do not want to do anything to offend them. People on your campaign committee must also realize that you are the one who is running and will make the ultimate decision. Sometimes supporters on campaign committees become offended when you do not accept their suggestions.

Make sure you have the look of a candidate. This is a

professional position in which you are the leader or CEO of a major corporation. Governments can sometimes have bigger budgets and more employees than any other business in your area. How you present yourself to the public is very important to show that you have leadership abilities and are capable of running a major business. This presentation of yourself has many parts including how you dress, your physical appearance, how you talk, how you carry yourself, and even your hygiene, to mention a few. I had to make a lot of changes in my lifestyle. I have worn a uniform my entire life and preferred when I was off to be in shorts and a t-shirt, but that just will not work on most campaign trails.

If you are not familiar with proper business attire and business casual dress, there is nothing wrong. Wearing a suit to work on a daily basis is not what everybody in America does and people realize that, but they also want to see that you have the ability to appear as a professional business leader. Find a trusted friend or confidant who can help you choose the proper attire for specific events. Several comfortable suits and the ability to wear them correctly goes a long way. Sometimes you will be invited to formal events that you may have not been exposed to before. Again, there is no shame in reaching out to research the proper etiquette in such situations. Ask the person inviting you or call to find out what the dress is for the event. Black tie, formal, business, or business casual are usual good reference points. There is nothing worse than going to a formal event where you have potential contributors who notice that you are uncomfortable in recognizing some of the formal processes to go along with dining events. The internet has made finding information easy to help us with almost anything. It has been a long time since my high school prom, so I had to watch several YouTube videos on the proper way to wear a tuxedo and even ordered the entire thing and had it delivered in two days for the price of renting it twice. I've worn it several times, and they sure are different from the purple velvet of 1982.

A candidate should always look as if they are fresh and ready to go. You should never have that appearance of being worn out and should always smile. It almost seems impossible, but you have to remember that you are marketing yourself and your name. You are the person who has to be sold to other people. Your first contact with a potential voter may be your only contact with that person, and you need to make the best impression possible. Even if it is a quick handshake, small talk, or just having someone see you, you must be at your best every time. Among political advisers there are many tricks to the trade. One of the techniques I was told was to always wear a long-sleeved button-down shirt all the time. Of course, you need to make sure that the shirt is clean and well pressed, but if the occasion presents itself, roll your sleeves up and get to work. The long sleeves give that professional look and when you get ready to work, or at least appear to get to work, roll up the sleeves just enough. I know they can be hot—I live in Florida—but make it look natural and wear a plain white t-shirt underneath to absorb sweat and look professional. Ladies may also wear long sleeves and business attire, but I would skip the white Hanes t-shirt.

Another hint given to me by several political advisers is that facial hair on men has the appearance that the candidate is hiding from something. Now, I've seen several candidates with beards and goatees win elections, but the fact is that most in the political arena are clean-shaven and a neat. I started growing a light beard while campaigning and was told this by one of my advisers. I shaved the next morning and never grew out facial hair again while I was actively running. I did not win that election, but I still did not take the chance during the next one.

Finally, make sure you have good manners and hygiene. Be ready to shake hundreds of hands, and if you suffer from chronic sweaty palms or have bad breath, do something to try to fix this. Keep something in your pocket to wipe your hand off and always keep some type of breath mint that you can hide in your mouth so people don't know you have it in there and can talk well. You don't want to chew gum when you're talking or pop it, and definitely make sure you do not have body odor. Finally, if you are not an etiquette genius, watch some videos on proper eating techniques so you know what fork to use, how to place a napkin properly in your lap, and hopefully you know not to eat with your mouth open or talk with food in your mouth. I know these things seem to be common sense, but you would be amazed by the number of people running for office who need to read this.

After you get your slogan and professional attire, get professional-looking photos of yourself so you can put them on a palm card or a business card. The photo should be a headshot of yourself that is very clear and in color. I personally used a picture of myself and my dog on all my pictures. I remember people later asking me how my dog was doing, and I think that contributed to them remembering me. Calling cards are postcard or bigger sized advertisements where you put information about you and your campaign. Hand these out to as many people as you can; this is your way of introducing yourself and giving them something physical that they can read about you later. You want to include a phone number and also a website that they can go to. Facebook, Twitter, Instagram, and other social media logos also let people know where they can find you on social media. Make sure that your name is bold, and that no matter what, they see your name. Even if they don't read the rest of the card, your name was imprinted in their brain. Remember, you're selling your name because that is what they're going to see on the ballot. I personally used business cards with my name on the front, and a third of the back was taken up with my picture and then a few details about me. These were very inexpensive and I was able to purchase thousands of these, which I could leave at any spot that would get attention. I remember driving up to a large convenience store and seeing my cards with my name on every gas pump and later finding out that these were placed by supporters every time they would stop. I don't know if it helped or not, but every person getting gas looked at my name for the five-plus minutes they were there pumping gas. If all twelve pumps had a card put on them, then the most that was spent on this advertisement was probably ten cents. I'm sure the cards were thrown away or blew off, but I got name recognition for that short period of time.

Make sure that you keep the calendar of events and appointments that you have. Keep your deadlines on the calendar and reach out to find out when political organizations meet and when there are events with large numbers of people that you can be exposed to. This is one of the most important things in a campaign because you will lose track of time, and events will start to blend into each other. Events will be covered in detail in chapter nine, but remember you cannot make everything.

# Chapter 8

# The Opposition

The best-case scenario is that in an election you will not run opposed. This means there is nobody running against you, and therefore it makes the campaign process easier. This usually does not happen and you may have one or more people running against you for the position. Never stop campaigning, even if you do not have an opponent. Until the closing time for an opponent to put their name on the ballot, you could still have competitors enter the race. Your opponent may enter the race just hours before closing time to get their names on the ballot. There are a variety of reasons for their delay, and less time to campaign may hurt their chances, but the last thing you want to do is get caught off guard. This happens many times to the incumbent, or person who is already in office, and who has been in office for several terms and has run unopposed in the past. This newcomer may not actually be a strong contender but can definitely cost a lot of money and cause a lot of work, especially when the incumbent is not prepared.

The incumbent is a person who currently holds the position. An incumbent is going to be your toughest opposition in a race because they have already been elected to the position and usually have some type of name recognition. Even if this name recognition is not always positive, it is still on the minds of voters, even if they do not know why. There is a saying in politics, "Even bad news is news." This means that even if the news is not great, it is news and the person's name is getting out there. Being an incumbent has both good and bad qualities. The positive part of being an incumbent is that hopefully they have done something good in the past term that they can use to campaign with. The negative part is that they have probably made a vote that people do not agree with or have done something that offends people during their term which can also be used against them.

You must research your incumbent's voting record and everything they have done or not done over the past term. If the position has recorded meetings, you should review these meetings or have one of your team do so and find highlights that can be utilized during the campaign. Screen shots of live videos are good sources of negative pictures of your opponent, if you want to go that way. The incumbent is also going to be more experienced about the job position, and this may be a disadvantage for you. Use caution when getting into details about subjects you are not familiar with or allowing the incumbent opposition to bait you. They have been living the position the last few years and will most likely be much more experienced in the details of certain government matters. Make sure to learn as much about the position as possible to help you.

Opposition research on either an incumbent or another newcomer running against you is critical. You must learn everything about them to help you compete with them. If there are videos or you have personal knowledge of their speaking abilities, make sure you are familiar with it. You should also find out everything about the person including the same information that you have vetted on yourself. This information may be difficult to obtain without assistance, but a regular public records check online and a review of their social media is an invaluable tool. Make sure that you look for your opponent's friends on social media so you can recognize them in an audience. It is not uncommon for an opponent to put a staged person at an event who asks you questions to try to throw you off or make you look bad. If you recognize the person, there is no shame in finding a polite way of mentioning that they are a friend of your opponent.

Going negative against your opponent in a campaign is a difficult decision for most. Once you start a negative campaign, you can expect the same in return. Usually, the first time an opponent goes negative is the only time that their opposition is surprised. After that, they're going to be on the defense. Negatives can be done in person during speeches but are most likely done in media. There are many marketing techniques for doing negative media on a candidate, but caution should be used. One common warning is a male going negative against a female opposition candidate. It could appear as if someone was picking on the female, and even though we are in a society of equal gender, it still may have a negative effect. I heard of this happen when a male incumbent mentioned a female opposition's bankruptcy and financial issues, only to have it backfire on him when she stated that she was a single mother struggling in a bad economy. The incumbent had a legitimate reason to bring up the matter because the opponent originally questioned his experience in finance, and he replied with her inability to handle her personal finances. No matter what the issue was, it looked bad for the incumbent, and he later lost. Whether this was a reason or not, negative attacks on a female, and at that meeting, were obviously not taken well.

The top priority when dealing with your opposition is to never use his or her name. As stated throughout this book, your main function is to market yourself and your name to the potential voters. The thing they need to remember is your name, which will be what they see on the ballot. The last thing you want to do is continually mention your opponent's name and give him or her free advertising. You also want to minimize any titles that your opponent has. If your opponent is the current mayor of the town, you do not want to refer to him or her as Mayor Jones, you simply refer to them as "my opponent." The same goes if they carry another title such as "Doctor" or any other recognizable title. Depending on the area, some elections allow titles to be placed on the ballot, and mentioning this would make them even more recognizable. I have not read any legal requirement in my fifty-four years on this planet that states you must address someone by their title, but it is a form of respect. The respect is for the title they earned, but you do not have to refer to them by title if you do use their name. This can have positive or negative effects and must also be thought out thoroughly. The best-case scenario is that you address your opponent, Dr. Jones, as Mr. Jones, and he corrects you and says, "That's Dr. Jones." People may think the doctor believes he is above others or they may think the person not calling them by their deserved title is disrespectful. Also, not pronouncing your opponent's name correctly can have the same effects, but on psychologically, it shows that they are insignificant. This is easy to get away with when your opponent has a difficult name, but if you mispronounce a simple name, it may make you look uneducated. My last name is Gold, simple and like the color. I had an opponent call me Gould; I knew the strategy and was amused when someone called him out and said, "His name is Gold, just like it is spelled." Keep focused. You are there to sell your name and your name only.

# Chapter 9

# **Events**

I hope that you are a member of several different civic, nonprofit, or community organizations prior to running for office. Joining your local party affiliation's clubs and going to events prior to announcing your run for office is invaluable, especially if you have had several years of attendance. Community organizations and other the business groups are a great way to get your name out among those who vote and contribute to elections. Joining these organizations is always best to do prior to running for office, because many times people running for office only show up when they are running and this offends people, especially those who are longtime members of political party organizations or clubs. Additionally, being a member of a political party and going to meetings prior to running gives you insight into other political figures and candidates. You will also meet some of the people who are official and unofficial leaders in the party. Remember, one good supporter can get you five or more votes. The supporters vote, and their family and friends voting for you may all be a result of one person. For the past four decades I have had people call me and ask who I thought was best in particular elections; for that reason I made sure I found people who get the same calls and made sure they knew me.

There are many events that will align with your political party or are political in nature that you should attend. Those who belong to political organizations are most likely to show up to vote. Even if you were not part of these clubs prior to your campaign, you should attend these regularly and make sure that you get to the meetings early and stay late to speak with those in attendance. Attend meetings yourself and do not send somebody else in your place. A hint about going to these meetings is to make sure that you know the Pledge of Allegiance, and always have a prayer ready in case you are asked to lead with one. I've seen candidates running for office who, either through nervousness or from being put in front of a group, forgot the words to start the Pledge of Allegiance and others who have stumbled through a basic prayer when they were called to lead the group.

You should also be educated in the office you are running for and the various structures of government. Be ready for any question and do not make up answers you don't know. If you are even just thinking about running for an office in the future, find some of these meetings and go to them. Take a few dollar bills for the club or committee raffles or 50/50 if they have them, and simply say you want to learn more about the organization. Word spreads quickly even if you just say you are looking at running.

Civic and community clubs and organizations are great places to get your name out, but if you are running in an election in which you have to focus on one particular party to get the vote, remember these are non-partisan, and members may not even vote. With that said, these organizations are great to be a part of especially if you join far in advance of announcing your political aspirations. They do great things for your community and you will meet a wide array of community and political leaders who know the importance of belonging to these organizations.

Even if you are not part of a civic or community organization such as Rotary, Kiwanis Club, or any of the various business clubs, you can be invited to speak at them if you reach out to someone in the leadership or have a friend who is a current member. Many of these groups like to hear from candidates to help decide who to vote for, but make sure to take a one dollar bills with you because many have a raffle or some type of dollar fundraiser that you will want to participate in. If you really want to impress them, donate the money back to the club if you win.

One word of caution, these groups will many times ask you to join, and the fees can be very high. If you do not have the money personally to do it and have to resort to using campaign funds, if applicable by law, think about whether or not it is the best way to spend money that can be used for advertisements. Also, you will be constantly asked to donate to various charitable organizations and other groups while you are running. Keep your focus and remember where you need to put your dollars. If allowed by law in your area, campaign funds can be returned to the contributors after an election. These unused funds are usually returned through a process of an overall percentage rate to avoid irregularities. The unused funds can also be donated to charities, and they will usually send you a letter at the end of your campaign. Consult with your local laws in reference to this.

One group that I will definitely recommend if you are not a strong speaker is Toastmasters International. This not only gives you speaking experience but also puts you in a group of others from your community. Public speaking will be one of the most important parts of your campaign and you need to feel comfortable with it if you are not currently used to speaking in front of groups of people. The one thing I've learned about Toastmasters is that they will tell you straight. If you want to go somewhere and have them tell you that you're wonderful and great and not get critiqued, this is probably not the place for you, but then again but you should think twice about running if you are not thick-skinned and cannot handle the negative side.

Take the opportunity to put your name out as many times as possible. You can do this in several ways through marketing at events. When you attend meetings or go anywhere in public, you can wear a badge that you can have made for between $10 and $20 with your name and what you are running for. I personally bought several inexpensive long-sleeved button-down and polo shirts and had my name embroidered on them with what position I was running for. I had my name embroidered in a color that stood out against the color of the shirt, and my name was in larger letters so that people could read it or see it even if they did not read what I was running for, which was embroidered underneath my name. I had long-sleeved shirts for more formal events and polo shirts for business casual events or even outdoor events that were less casual. I wore the shirts everywhere I went including to the store, restaurants, and anywhere else where I knew people would be. I had t-shirts made, but rarely wore them unless it was a very casual event like a 5k for charity or something like that. If you have a business or work for a company that allows your name on your shirt, have that name enlarged so people can easily read it. It is advertising your name that gets you noticed, so think of anything that is easily done at a low cost. Remember, this is a form of random marketing, and you are just hoping that a voter sees your name and remembers it.

Pick your events wisely. At times you will notice that you see the same people at every event. Weigh the benefits of going to an event that has the same people you see every time versus going to another event that has a new group. Even if you go to an event that only has a couple of people, you still showed up and showed that you cared enough to go there. Sometimes there are more candidates at events than there are people there to hear them. Don't be discouraged and continue to go because you know that if you miss it, you will be ridiculed by your opponent.

# Chapter 10

# Marketing

In most elections you will never meet every voter, and they will most likely not know you or even understand the position you are running for. The majority of voters are not educated as to what items and what positions are open on a ballot. This means that you need to get your name out so that they are exposed to your name multiple times prior to voting. Therefore, you are marketing a name just the same as you would market any product that you would find at your local grocery store.

One of the most interesting classes I had when I started my first doctoral program was Marketing Management. Product placement is a technique of putting actual products or product names in areas that are seen on television, at the movies, sporting events, or anywhere there are people. Many times they are done subtlety and sometimes they are blatant, as with enlarging the brand name on a soda can or on a computer so the viewer sees it. One of the best examples of product placement was in a scene from one of my favorite movies when the leading actor and his cohort walk out of an office after getting chewed out for doing a flyby and run into a person carrying coffee on a tray. The coffee spills on another cast member and there is a quick glimpse of a soft drink manufacturer's name and logo on the tray that is probably only visible for a split second, but you see it. Why a soldier would be carrying coffee on a tray with a soft drink company's name and logo on it in a military facility probably doesn't even register to most people. It did not register with me the first ten or twenty times I saw the movie, but after taking Marketing Management, I saw it along with many other product placements throughout this movie and other places every day. Why do you think major corporations pay millions of dollars to get their names on sports arenas and stadiums? Getting your name visible and heard is what you want to do, and you want people to see it and remember it. Your name needs to be familiar to them even when they do not remember why it is familiar, so when they see it on that ballot it sticks out to them and they vote for you.

The next question you want to ask is, "How do I get my name out to everybody?" You most likely will not have the advertising budget of a major soft drink company or a computer company named after a specific fruit. The answer is simple—targeted marketing. Unlike regular marketing where you have to target a vast group that may have no interest in buying your product, in elections you know who your target audience is, and many times you know exactly who will be voting. Your elections official will have data from prior elections which will show you a variety of information that is extremely valuable to you or your campaign adviser. This information can include past turnout percentages, the number of voters for each political party, and it can even tell you by name the people who voted in the last election; it can also provide you with contact information, including their address, phone number, and even their email address. Before we dive into breaking down this information, there are some key terms that you should understand before making contact with any potential voter.

Voter: A voter is a person registered with an eligibility to vote in your election. With this in mind, why would you target somebody who's not eligible to vote or who is not voting in your election? This will make sense later in this chapter when we discuss television, radio, and other similar forms of marketing.

Super Voter: A person who votes in all elections in their area, usually over the last decade. This highly sought-after voter will show up to the polls to cast their vote no matter what the weather is or what type of election they're voting in. A super voter shows up to all primaries in special elections, even if there's only one thing on the ballot to vote for. You know that they are going to vote, and therefore you need to target them so that they know your name and vote for you.

General election: This is the final election that usually determines who will fill the role of the open position at the beginning of the next term. General elections usually include voters from all political parties and are open for anyone to vote. This is the election that, during a presidential election season, usually occurs the first week of November.

Primary elections: Elections that are held usually several months before the general election and are done to narrow down the candidates prior to the overall general election. The primary election usually includes a runoff of those in the same political party so that going into the general election there is only one person representing each political party. For example, if there are five Democrats and five Republicans running for the same position, there would be a primary election to narrow the field down to one Democrat and one Republican who would go into the general election. This field would increase if there were other political parties running in the same election.

The primary elections and understanding their importance is something that many novice candidates or campaign managers miss. They forget the importance of winning the primaries and don't get that if the candidate does not win the primary, there is no going forward. This is why it is very important to research and find the voters to target for the primary election separate from the general election. In essence, you are actually running two campaigns. The first part is the concentration on the primary election and if you win the primary, then you conduct another election for the general election.

Throughout my career I've had people invite me to events that I knew were a mix of all parties or had very few of the political party members that I was concentrating on. For the purpose of giving an example, let's say that I am running for mayor of a town and I am a Democrat. I have two other Democratic challengers, which I must face off against in August during a primary election. It is now July and I'm pushing to meet as many Democratic voters as possible, and my campaign manager has suggested that I go to a local

Republican club meeting prior to my primary election. Yes, this may be a good idea in case I win my primary election and then I will need some of the Republican votes, but when time is limited it is best to concentrate your time on where you know the voters are going to be. This all comes with experience and knowing where your voters are. Additionally, you should also determine which special interest groups you should focus on and if they have party affiliations. A simple internet search will help you identify groups to concentrate on.

This section is probably going to be the most important area of the entire book and will have a follow-up in chapter 11. This is where I explain the importance of mailers. Even though I had been associated with multiple campaigns for several decades, I never understood the importance of campaign mailers until I ran for office. When I was told during my first campaign that I would need $50,000 just for mailers, I thought my adviser was crazy, but now I wish I had $100,000 to put in. I said nobody reads those things, they just throw them away—his reply was, "How else are you going to get your name in the hands of the people you know are voting for you?"

The best way to describe mailers is that you know exactly who your voters are. You know who are the registered voters and you know which ones will be voting in your upcoming election. If you are in an open election or race, you have to target everyone. If you are in a closed election or race, you only have to target your party voters. You have to target these people, and there is no other way to get into their homes and into their hands other than a piece of paper that is sent through the good old United States Postal Service. I know exactly what you're saying at this point—you'd never read junk mail. Most people don't, but how do you know it's junk mail until you look at it? This is why the creation of your mailer is the most important strategy of your entire campaign. Chapter 11 will go further into this subject and tell you why you have to win this eight-second ride.

*Signs*

Signs, signs and more signs littering the streets as far as you can see. I hate political signs. Most people think this is how you win an election, and I am sure some have. As mentioned above and will be discussing in the next chapter, your mailers are the best way to target voters in an election unless you can talk to every single voter. Signs, like most over forms of media, are the shotgun effect of advertising. You fire a shot and hope one of the pellets hits the target. To go even further, for you hunters out there, you can also look at it like buckshot and birdshot. Double-aught buckshot has eight pellets, whereas birdshot has around one hundred or more per ounce. We will use that comparison with big signs and little signs.

Signs are not free. A common double-sided yard sign is around $5 with the metal stands. Large 4'x8' signs, which you will need if you expect someone to read them going by at 35 mph or more, will cost you anywhere from $25 to $50 or more per one-sided panel. Plus, you will need to build a large frame for these large signs with legs long enough to go about twenty-four inches into the ground, and I always suggest painting the frames to match your signs so they always look more professional. Two one-sided signs to a frame, so that when the sun is out, which is about the only time you will see them, people will not see the other side coming through, which could create a big blur. Use good, wide head tacks or short nails to put the signs on so they do not blow off. Altogether you can expect to pay about $100 for these large signs.

The size of your community and election will vary, and the number of signs will too. If it is a local election, you will need to concentrate on your area, but if it is a statewide or federal election, it would be almost impossible to put signs everywhere. The area I live in is large geographically—over 1,600 square miles—and has just under a quarter-million registered voters for a population closing in on 350,000. I usually put out approximately twenty to twenty-five signs, which is a small number compared to others in my area, but I always have people telling me they see my signs everywhere.

I move my signs around and have the most dedicated and organized person you will ever find who puts my signs out. He finds the best high-traffic areas, and he builds bases that allow the signs to be moved. Throw a couple sandbags on them and you have a corner lot sign that you can move to the other side, even on a daily basis. These work well on any property because at night you can move them and people see them everywhere, plus you can touch them up and they look new. I am sure if you want to pay David Woolf, he will come to you, especially if you live in the mountains or on the beach, but only in my non-election season.

I always try to buy local when it comes to campaigning

because many times, these local merchants are your supporters. I especially do this when it comes to campaign signs because you can actually talk to someone face-to-face and hopefully see some of their past work. I used a local company that does not outsource the work and makes the signs locally, which is rare. Their sole business is making signs and they also do most of the real estate signs in the area, which gives them a lot of experience making quality signs that will last and not fade. I have seen signs that you know someone ordered from an online print source, and these signs fade weeks into an election, the print is not aligned correctly, or there are a variety of other low-quality errors. Remember, these signs are printed on lightweight corrugated plastic and you need them to last months, maybe even years if you run again. My signs are going on eight years and look as fresh as when I got them and will continue to as long as I store them properly.

On the design process, remember your name is what you want out there. Many people want or think they need their picture on a sign, and for some it is an advantage but for others, well, you know. You do not see the picture on the ballot, only the name. If your look is so good that it makes people remember you, then go for it. There are also requirements in reference to the design of the sign that may necessitate disclaimers and other information, and these vary by area. Additionally, there may be state laws and county and city ordinances that regulate locations and times that signs may be put out and taken down. In most areas there are regulations on when the signs must be taken down after an election, and you could be fined for each sign not taken down. Make sure to have someone write down where each sign is to make sure you get them down, and this includes yard signs.

Use a color pattern that sticks out with good contrasting colors, and if you have a slogan that is short and catchy enough, put it on there, but it is, for the hundredth time, your name you need people to see as they drive by your sign. It is that short glimpse that they need to file away that counts. I used two sets of signs in one election and will most likely do it again. I am superstitious about things, or at least I am scared not do something again, so I will use both, but I already have them from the last two elections. I suggest not using two different signs because it may confuse people. A good internet search of "political signs" with the image option always helps, plus you get to see some pretty funny ones too.

*Yard Signs*

Yard signs should be designed in the same manner as to color, name dominance, and required political disclaimer information on them. These should be two-sided and need to be the same quality as the large signs. Yard signs are a necessity, not as much for winning the election, but to make your supporters feel good. Many times these signs cause more problems when overzealous supporters place them in areas where they do not have permission or on the right-of-way. You need to have permission to put a sign on someone's property, and it is common for candidates or their supporters to place them on vacant land, in front of businesses or government properties, or mostly along the right-of-way or side of the road. Placing a sign on someone's property is like trespassing and then posting that you did it. It offends people when you post a sign without permission and loses votes. Also, make sure you have the owner's permission and not just the people who work in a business or the manager. Many larger businesses and many businesses in general do not outwardly support candidates because it may cause them to lose customers, especially in a heated race. Many businesses rent or lease their space and the property owner may not want any signs there.

Signs placed on improper properties usually get thrown away, so there goes $5 that you could have used to send a mailer to ten or more people you know will be voting. Hopefully, no one will line a busy intersection right-of-way with a row of ten signs in each direction, which I have seen. Forty yard signs all on the right-of-way were placed by a candidate one year, and within hours the local authorities responsible for keeping the right-of-way clear picked them up and placed them in a dumpster at the landfill. I could definitely find a better way of using $200 than hoping people on their way to work on a Monday morning were more interested in my signs than planning their week after the weekend. Luckily for those in my area, the local government's code enforcement group that picks up improperly placed signs puts them all in one clean dumpster at the county landfill, and candidates or their designees are allowed to go there and retrieve them. Check your local state laws and county or city ordinances in reference to sign placement and remember, you can be fined for improper sign placement—whether you physically placed the sign or not, it is your election and your name.

Yard signs make your supporters feel good, and most people think that the best way to support you is to put a sign in their yard. In a way, it is, but they also don't realize that these signs are not free. When you are in a political race that you know will cost you upwards of $100k in mailers alone, the last thing you want to do is buy 1,000 yard signs that you know will end up in the garbage. I once had a friend of mine call me and ask me for twenty yard signs, and I told him that I was short on signs, but I could get him a few if he wanted to place them in front of his business, which was a very busy and popular restaurant in a high turnout election precinct area—an extra bonus. He said, "No, I want them for my house. We are having a sign war in my neighborhood and I want to put a bunch in my yard." I said, "I can get them to you, but that's $100 worth of signs and I need them for the campaign." His response was, "I thought they were free." After a few minutes' discussion over the fact that nothing is free and how campaigning works, I did tell him he could have one for his yard and one for his business. The sign never made it up at the restaurant, and I'm not sure if he won his sign war, but it is surprising how many people think things are free in an election. It is hard to tell someone to buy a sign or to contribute to your campaign to get one, but it is easier to tell them that you are running low on signs and you're raising funds for a new order, then see if they take the hint to help. If not, give them a sign and be happy they are supporting you. I have given away many a sign that I am sure never made it out of the trunk of the car, but at least they said they would vote for me.

## *Where and How Many Yard Signs?*

As with anything, the more you buy, the better discount you usually get, but you also do not want signs left over. This is how I calculate my yard sign purchase: I take the number of election precincts and multiply it by two because in each precinct there will be a physical location for people to cast their votes. I want a couple signs there so someone sees my name before entering. Then I double this number, which gives me a guideline as to how many to buy at first. To make it simpler, if I have 136 precincts, I round it up to 150, then multiply that times two. That is 300, then I double it which gives me 600. The sign maker will probably tell you that it will be cheaper to buy 1,000, but try for 750. Do the math—if you do not need them, in the end it cost you more. Every dollar spent on a sign is two mailers lost to someone who you know will vote. Remember to save the signs for the precincts at the beginning so you're not scrambling at the end. Also, look at your data and see how many people show up to each precinct. One of the precincts in my area has fewer than twenty people who are registered to vote in my closed primary election. I actually mailed each one of them one of my mailers with a handwritten note in lieu of driving an extra twenty miles and putting up the sign the voting location. I'm not sure if that is what worked, but in the end, I won that precinct.

## *Billboards*

After my negative rant on signs, I'm sure you are thinking you are going to hear the same about billboards. Of course, billboards are less effective than directly mailing voters or speaking face-to-face to them, but they do come in ahead of several other forms of media in my opinion. Billboards are expensive, but if properly selected and designed, they can be an effective way of reaching out to voters, especially those non-super voters and the ones you cannot reach out to by mail. Your primary consideration when looking at billboards is the location. You want to find a location that has the highest traffic count and preferably at a location where cars are stopped while waiting for a traffic light. Additionally, you want to have it be an area that is most visible to local traffic in lieu of an interstate or toll road that would have many out-of-town visitors. I prefer to use the digital or electronic billboards for several reasons. Primarily, you can change your "screen" on the billboard if you want to change the message, plus there are no art fees if you use a digital design. The sign maker I used also provided me with the digital designs at no extra fee. You are able to put multiple designs on the electronic billboards, which can sometimes catch the attention of the reader more.

As I said, I had two designs for my signs due to support from the local firefighters. I posted both sign designs on my billboard, which changed every ten seconds with other advertisements. It worked out that I received extra time on the board with the two designs and did not pay anything more because when there are fewer advertisers, your time will run longer. I picked a major road that was the main entrance to two of the largest employers in my area and was able to rent the space for the month prior to my primary election. I got this idea and the traffic data from a friend of mine who owned a fast food restaurant and the billboard above it. They did an in-kind contribution for space on their sign, and I saw the value when I met people who told me they did not know I was running until they saw the sign.

Be cautious when opting to get a billboard that is not electronic or digital. They may cost less per month and give you a longer contract, but you may have a price to pay for artwork or for the transfer of the image, plus they may be more difficult to see at night. Depending on your area and the location of the sign, the prices will vary dramatically. I paid over $1,000 for one month and again, it is not a direct marketing tool. The salesperson may give you a figure showing you the value per contact, but remember, you know which voters you are looking for and you know how to get to them.

*Social Media, Radio, Television, Magazines, and Newspapers*

I have a lot of friends in all these industries, and it is always hard when they call me to give me that "first chance" at the $1,500 quarter-page ad or prime radio time. Social media, streaming music, and things such as podcasts have almost eliminated some of these media sources. I will not go into detail about the disadvantages of each, just remember who your target audience is. I don't know the last time I've actually read the print version of my local newspaper or even thumbed through a magazine at my doctor's office. With mobile devices and the internet, you can take your newspaper and even your magazine with you anywhere you want. Though most news media sources offer online and digital formats, many people still get their news, whether real or fake, from social media. As stated earlier, after the 2016 elections, social media is regulating how political information is delivered. Each social media venue has different rules for political opinion and advertisements and should be researched individually. Social media is a valuable source that also allows you to target specific groups, but still not as specific as meeting with or reaching out to the voter by mail.

# Chapter 11

## **Eight Seconds**

Like a rodeo event, you only have seconds to win your event. You either stay on or you get thrown off at the chute, which means better luck next time. This "eight second" saying is another Jeffism I came up with to describe mailers. You only have a few seconds from the time someone takes your mailer out of the mailbox and decides to look at it or toss it. Either way, they have seen your name and that is the goal. Hopefully, your mailer will make the coveted "save" pile and not get thrown in the recycle bin. This is where you must make sure that your mailer gets their attention and imprints your name in their memory.

Obviously, I am a true believer in mailers and no, I do not own a print company or a mail sorting business. You just have to look at this logically to see the benefit of using mailers for your campaign. Though we are in a digital world of email and mobile phones, we still get mail, sometimes referred to as snail mail due to its lack of speed, sent to us in one form or another. Hopefully we check our mail daily for those bills that we still don't get online or looking for that $5 bill in a birthday or Christmas card from Aunt Millie, but either way we always check our mail. There is no other form of media that ensures delivery to the voter other than the US Post Office. The trick to it is making sure that your design primarily imprints your name so that the voter remembers it. If you've made it through the chute and are still holding on, you want your mailer to further impress the voter so that they remember to look for your name and not just hope that they recognize it.

Your mailer design must be able to catch the attention of the voter in that short time that they pull it out of the mailbox and sort between coupons, pizza delivery, and all the other political mailers. When that voter, or more importantly that super voter, unloads their mailbox with half a dozen or more other political advertisements, you want yours to catch their eye. Even if it is just seeing your name and causing them to remember it, you have done your job. There is a science to creating mailers and a large number of do's and don'ts that go along with their creation.

If you have never designed a mailer or have little experience in producing them, this is the point where I'd suggest that you get the professional help of a campaign manager or adviser. I am fairly computer literate, but for the time it takes and the potential errors, it is better to get a person who is good at computer design. The first thing to do is to make sure that this person will sign a confidentiality agreement and not take on your opponent as a client. In my first campaign the production of mailers and distributing them was almost like being in a spy movie. My campaign adviser designed the mailers and utilized a commercial printing company that advertises on television to print mass numbers of business cards, flyers, banners and other items. He did not want to use any local companies, both due to the price difference and also the fear that information would leak to my opponent.

Once the designs were made we had to find a mass mail distributor that was capable of sending out the tens of thousands of mailers and to get them to their destinations on a specific date. I watched my campaign adviser question the owner of the mass mail distributor as to what other clients they had and what type of security was done on the building at night. He even went as far as to request that any misprints or damaged mailers be returned to us to ensure that they do not get put into the garbage. The reason for this is that someone on my opponent's campaign could do a nighttime dumpster-diving expedition to see what we are putting out. This may seem ridiculous, but what if your opponent was getting ready to put out a negative mailer on you—wouldn't you want to know about it to counter it?

If you do not have a budget to send a mailer out to everyone who is going to vote in your election, first concentrate on super voters who will be voting in your election. Make sure that the mailers are sent out several days prior to the polls opening or as close to the same day in which an absentee ballot is received in the mail. It may take sending out several different mailers to get the attention of the voter. I sent out approximately half a dozen separate mailers in each of the two elections I ran in. Remember, you are selling your name!

I never would have believed in the use of mailers until I had people specifically comment and ask about one of my mailers. As I mentioned in a previous chapter about having a picture with my dog on all my campaign cards, I also used the same picture on my mailers. This picture was so popular that later I had people asking me how my dog was and remembering him by name. I asked them how they knew about it, and they said they saw it on my mailer and that is why they voted for me. I knew who my target was and I sent them something that caught their attention.

Mailers are costly and can run around fifty cents to several dollars each to produce, label, sort, and send out. The largest cost is the postage, and depending on how many you send out, you want the best bulk rate deal you can get. Ten thousand mailers is usually where you get the best price in all aspects of service, including the bulk rate fee, plus a lot of mail distributors require this number as a minimum. I strongly suggest using a distributor who can print the names on your mailers, along with bar codes and any other mailing requirements. A good mail distributor will also have the software available to take out duplicate addresses and print the addressee the way you want it.

It is not uncommon for there to be several registered voters living in one location. With the average mailer costing around $1, you do not want to send a mailer to everybody in the household, as this is a waste of money. This is why you use a mail distributor that can cut out duplicate addresses and only have one mailer sent to each address instead of sending one to each person at the address. Additionally, there is nothing that restricts you from going through the list of voters and taking out names that you do not need to mail something to. I contributed a lot of my own money to my first campaign and needed to cut the cost down as much as I could. Even though my list of potential voters were in the tens of thousands, I still went through every one and cut names of those I knew already supported me and those who I knew would not vote for me. I knew that the average for each mailer was approximately fifty cents, so for every name I cut out, I saved that amount of money to use on future mailers or to send to other groups that may not have been on the super voter list. Even if you have a large base of contributors, I still think it is financially responsible for you or one of your team members to go through these lists and make sure there are no duplicates or names that do not need a mailer.

There are several ways of addressing your potential voter. You can use the official name registered to vote or you can use a generic title like, "Voter at the address of..." I personally choose the first line to say, "The Jackson Family" or whatever the name of the residents is. Sometimes you will run across multiple different last names at the same address, which may be a situation to use the title, "To the Registered Voters." In my opinion, any way you can customize or personalize mailers, the more they will be noticed.

## Chasing the Absentees

"Chasing the absentees" is a common phrase used in the world of political campaigns. Absentee voters are those who cannot be present to go to the voting polls on the day of the election or during early voting, if allowed in your area. These voters will request an absentee ballot which will be mailed to them shortly before the election, but with enough time to return them and be counted. These ballots can be mailed to anywhere in the world, including the US military. If a voter is not in the same geographical area, bulk rate postage will not be allowed. Also, if there are not enough absentee voters to make the bulk rate minimum, regular first class postage will be required, depending on the size of the mailer. Getting your information to absentee voters is as important as getting it to super voters. One might also consider that they are more important to send a mailer to because they are using the US Post Office and its service to cast their ballot, so you know they read their mail.

Many areas are now allowing voting by mail as an alternative to voting in person. This should be considered just as important as the absentee ballot because they have requested it to be sent by mail. Your goal is to get your mailer to the absentee or vote-by-mail requestor the same day or a day before they receive their ballot. Your goal is for them to see your name and information and choose you as the best candidate while they are filling out their ballot. There are also voters who request a mail ballot because they are in another country but remain US citizens and want to cast a vote. When sending a mailer to these potential voters, the postage will be at a much higher rate than regular first class mail. Several of the mail distributors I have dealt with in the past do not send these out because it requires additional work on the part of their employees or they charge a substantially higher amount to send these out. I have always handled these myself or had team members specifically for handling foreign mailers. Once you receive the information, you simply address your mailer and take it to the post office to send it out. The numbers are usually not that high, but for me they had been productive. I've heard many people say it's not worth the money and time to send out mailers to fewer than 100 voters who are out of the country, but I do not think you would find one person who lost an election by just several votes who wouldn't want to rethink this process.

In some areas, absentee and vote-by-mail requests may come out daily just before an election. Check with your mail distributor to see if they can handle these lists or be ready yourself or develop a team that can physically address the mailers and send them out daily by the US Postal Service. You most likely will not be able to receive bulk rate for these mailers, and it is a good practice to have several hundred stamps in reserve in case the data does not come out until the end of the day. You will want to address these mailers and send them out immediately after you get the list. Many people fill out and return their ballots all in one day. You want to make sure that your mailer gets there the same day and not after they may have mailed in their ballot. Many people will ask whether you should continue to send out mailers even after the person requested an absentee ballot. This is a difficult question to answer, and even though most people send their ballot back in immediately, what if the person simply held onto the ballot until the last minute? I have also seen people show up to the voting precincts with their absentee ballots. As always, each area has different rules governing how these ballots are handled, but to be safe you should probably continue to send out your mailers until the election is over. To my knowledge, there are no election officials who will give out the information on whether or not a specific person has cast their ballot.

To sum up my opinion on mailers, they are the best media value because you are sending them directly to people you know will vote. Send mailers only to those who you know will potentially vote for you. Research everything you can on the internet and look at other candidates' mailers from the past. If you have opposition who has run for any office before, look at their mailers. Everything is riding on how your mailers look and how you get them out. Find out what color schemes are best and get plenty of pictures to work with. The most important thing is, if you have an extra $100, mail 100 extra mailers to super voters. It is a sure bet that money spent will go to those who vote.

# Conclusion

Hopefully, by now you have realized that there is much more to running for office or managing a political campaign. Moreover, I hope I did not discourage you from trying. There are so many things to learn, and this is just a beginning. There are other areas including polling, debates, and dirty campaign techniques that I have skipped for obvious reasons or that could be, like every chapter here, a book in itself. One area I saved in detail for last is having the support of your family, mostly your spouse or significant other. My wife Shawn has given me unconditional support through everything I have done, including both elections. The elections were as hard, if not harder, on her as they were on me. She was there for me through the good and the not so good. I hope everyone has someone like this in their life. No one knows what it is like to run for public office unless they have run themselves, and no one knows what it is like to be the spouse or significant other of someone running for public office unless they have been one.

Running for a political office can be one of the most exhilarating or disappointing things you will ever do in your life, depending on which side of the election you end up on. Not many people unsuccessfully run for office and come back for a second try, but I did. I came back for a second try and won, but I cannot guarantee you will have the same results. I learned so much the first time and got so close, I wondered what would have happened if I tried a few things differently or did some things I did not do before. As with life, I focused on areas in which I could achieve and not in the areas I could not change, and then put everything I had into it. The ups and downs of an election are physically and mentally draining in a manner that you would never imagine. I think if I had not tried again, it would have been one of those things in life that I looked back at with regret. There is only one way that you will ever find out if you will win an election and that is to try.

# About the Author

Jeff Gold is an elected official in Florida. He has spent his entire life in politics. Jeff's political roots include several elected officials including his grandfather, uncle, and mother who once worked for Ronald Reagan and worked tirelessly for the advancement of her political party. Jeff has also worked on multiple campaigns at various levels before running for office himself in 2012. He spent over thirty years in public safety as a firefighter-paramedic and lieutenant, then later as a supervisor in law enforcement. Jeff has associate degrees in both Fire Science and Emergency Medical Services, a Bachelor of Arts in Organizational Studies, a master's degree in Criminal Justice, and has extensive doctoral studies in marketing, business, healthcare management, and is currently finishing his doctorate in education. Jeff and his wife Shawn have five adult daughters; one granddaughter, Skylar Jane; another granddaughter, Kinsley, on the way; a rescue dog, Puzzle; and Joe the Cat that they rescued from a dumpster. Jeff and Shawn are both very active in their community as volunteers and business owners. Shawn, who is a nurse, also runs a nonprofit organization to advance arts and sciences.

# Contact Information

Jeff Gold is the CEO of GSA Services, Inc. GSA Services is a full-service training, logistics, and travel agency that specializes in public safety and military training. Jeff is available for consulting and public speaking on a variety of subjects. If you are a candidate, special interest group, or anyone interested in having Jeff present the information in this book in person, he can be reached at jeffgold@gsaservices.org. Presentations are tailored to your group.

Jeff and his group can also recommend political managers, consultants, and marketing agents at all campaign levels throughout Florida.

Please visit our website at gsaservices.org or visit us on Facebook at one of the following pages: So You Want to Run for Office?, GSA Services, Inc., or GSA Travel.